COLOSSIANS

The Visible God

José Young

Ediciones Crecimiento Cristiano

Young, José

Colossians : The visible God / José Young. - 1a ed . - Villa Nueva :
Crecimiento Cristiano, 2020.

48 p. ; 21 x 14 cm.

Traducción de: José Young.
ISBN 978-987-1219-42-1

1. Estudios Bíblicos. I. Título.
CDD 220.07

Colossians is a translation of the study guide «Colosenses» published by
Ediciones Crecimiento Cristiano, ISBN 978-950-9596-76-4.

© Ediciones Crecimiento Cristiano

1ª Edición inglés: Septiembre 2020
ISBN: 978-987-1219-42-1

Córdoba 419 - Villa Nueva - Cba. - Argentina

+54 9 353 491-2450

+54 9 353 481-0724

oficina@edicionescc.com

www.edicionescc.com

Ediciones Crecimiento Cristiano

edicionescc

Index

Introduction

Colossae was a small city of little importance in the Lycus valley about 16 km from Laodicea in what presently is Turkey. It grew in the shadow of two more important cities, Laodicea and Hierapolis, and presently nothing is left of it but ruins. It was about 180 km from Ephesus.

Philemon, a resident of the city, had a slave called Onesimus who escaped and fled. He met Paul in Rome and was converted. Later on, Paul sent Onesimus back to Colossae together with Tychicus (Colossians 4:7-9) with two letters: one for his owner Philemon and another for the church, which is the letter we are about to study.

Colossae is familiar to the Christian world due to this letter that Paul wrote to its church. Apparently at that time the church was threatened by false teaching and the majority of commentators believe that Paul's purpose was to warn the believers of the danger. He doesn't say much about the problem itself but spends much time presenting the solution: an adequate understanding of who Christ is, his work and our relationship with him.

This study is not based in one special version of the Bible. In fact, we hope you would use two or more versions in your reading and study. We repeat a very basic rule of Bible study: read the whole book a number of times. It is that reading that allows us to have a clear understanding of the message of the book.

The Bible versions used in this study are:

ESV The English Standard Version
NIV New International Version
RSV The Revised Standard Version

1 Paul's concern

⇨ Colossians 1:1-14

As is the case with more than half of his letters, Paul wrote this one in collaboration with another person.

Many feel that Paul had eye problems, and for that reason, when possible, he dictated his letters. Paul was a team worker and he always had others with him who helped him and received practical training.

When Luke described Paul's various missionary travels in Acts, he does not mention a visit to Colossae. It is very possible that Paul was in prison when he wrote this letter (4:10).

But if Paul had not been to Colossae, it is quite possible that some people from there were included among those mentioned in Acts 19:9, 11. So it is quite possible that the church was born through his testimony.

Paul learned about the situation of the church through Epaphras (v. 7).

Verses 1 and 2 serve as introduction and greeting, and have a form very similar to the beginning of his other letters. In the majority of them he includes a benediction similar to what we see in verse 2: "Grace and peace to you from God our Father."

1/ What would the "peace" Paul asks for them be? If it's the same as that mentioned in John 14:27, what characteristics would it have?

Paul thanks God for what he learned about the church.

2/ Taking in account what Paul says,
   a/ what was the church in Colossae like?

b/ what characteristics did they have which may be lacking in our churches?

Paul said that two reasons why he gave thanks to God were their demonstration of faith and love.

3/ Is it possible to cultivate these characteristics or are they an automatic fruit of the Gospel?

Paul says that it was their "hope" that motivated them to demonstrate an abundant love.

4/ What was their hope? Look at 1 Peter 1:3-5 also.

Paul Learned about the situation in Colossae from Epaphras.
5/ What do we learn concerning him from the following passages? Colossians 1:7, 8; 4:12, 13; Philemon 23.

Another aspect of this letter, which is common for Paul, is how he talks about his prayer for them. Paul was a true man of prayer, and when we examine his letters, we see that he had a long list of people and churches that he constantly prayed for. That explains, at least in part, his power as a minister of the Gospel.

Paul says that he asks God to give them a broad understanding of his will, with wisdom and spiritual comprehension.

6/ What would be the results of this comprehension? Make a list of them. (There are at least 6)

7/ What does it mean to "bear fruit" (v. 10)? There are two possible answers.

The position of Paul is that a healthy Christian life is the result of spiritual understanding. Still, a person could know what the Bible teaches and understand what God's will is, yet not have a life of fruit or a life full of the power of God.

8/ In this case, what is the problem and what is the solution?

It was very possible that the church at Colossae could face opposition and false teaching, and for that reason Paul expected that as the result of his prayer they would be strengthened… "for all endurance and patience" (RSV), "strengthened...so that you may have great endurance and patience." (NIV).

Paul states that we have been qualified to share in the inheritance of the saints and have been transferred to the kingdom of Christ, that is, we are citizens of the kingdom of God.

9/ What would be involved in being a citizen of God's kingdom?

Paul's prayers help us to pray for those things that really count: to ask for those profound changes in a life that result in spiritual maturity.

As we finish this lesson, we suggest that you take a bit of time to pray together. Pray like Paul did. Think of a specific person and ask our Father for that person. Ask for the essential elements that result in a fruitful life, full of the power of God. And consider how Paul's model can guide us in our personal prayers.

10/   What motive might you have, right now, to be thankful to God for?

2 Christology

⇨ Colossians 1:15-23

AChristian is, in first place and by the biblical definition, a follower of Jesus Christ. As a consequence, we need to be specialists in the knowledge of him. In the gospels we see his life and hear his voice. This passage describes his "...glory as of the only Son from the Father..." (John 1:14)

If we had to choose just one word to describe this passage it would be "relationship", since we can see here the relationship between Jesus Christ and God, the created universe and ourselves.

1/ Let's look first at what Paul says about the relationship between Jesus the man and God the Father.

a/ Make a list of what this passage says concerning the Jesus of the gospels and God, that is, the details that help us understand that relationship.

b/ What is your personal conclusion based on the information in this passage?

The word translated as "image" here does not mean simply the representation of something, but more it's manifestation. Both the Old and New Testaments insist that no one has ever seen God (1 Timothy 6:16), but we see him in Jesus Christ.

2/ Look for another passage in the New Testament that repeats the idea that in Christ we see the invisible God.

This passage also speaks of various aspects of the relationship between Christ and creation.

3/ Explain the following statements (version RSV). Whenever you can support your explication with other passages, do it.

a/ "...for in him all things were created..." (v. 16). But what of Genesis 1:1?

b/ "He is before all things..." (v. 17)

c/ "...all things were created...for him." (v. 16)

d/ "...in him all things hold together." (v. 17)

It is important to note that Jesus Christ is the Creator not only of the tangible universe, but also of the angels and other invisible powers. The terms "thrones, dominions, principalities and authorities" refer to a range of spiritual authorities that are barely mentioned in the Bible, like for example Daniel 10:13, 20, 21.

The Jehovah Witnesses say that verse 15 proves that Jesus was also created by God, since he is the first-born. But the following verses imply that "first-born" means more than simply "born before others". The term "birthright" used in Genesis 25 signifies the rights of the first-born.

4/ How do the following verses show that the term "first-born" has a broad significance? Genesis 25:33, Exodus 4:22 and Psalm 89:27. Note the use of the term in each case.

Up until now the passage has described Jesus Christ as the one who reveals the Father and who is creator of all things. From verse 18 on we see him as the one who reconciles, who creates peace.

There is no doubt that presently we are living in the midst of a cosmic conflict (Romans 8:20-22). Nothing in this world functions as it should. But by means of the cross, Christ dealt with the cause of the conflict, even though we do not yet see the final results.

We understand that by means of the cross, we have peace with God (verse 23 and Romans 5:1). But will there be "peace" with those who reject Christ, with the demons and Satan? Obviously, they are included among the "all things" of verse 20.

5/ What do you think? Support your answer with at least one other Bible text.

a/ Just what would this "peace", this "reconciliation", be between God and his enemies?

b/ What has the cross to do with this "peace"?

Just as Jesus Christ has preeminence (or birthright) over the first creation, he also has those rights in the second. Verse 18 describes his relation to the new creation.

6/ Explain how the figure of Jesus as the head of his church, helps us to understand our relationship with him.

Did you notice how the lens of Paul narrows his focus through this passage? Note the following progression:

- Christ, the origin of all things.
- Christ, who reconciles the universe.
- Christ, who reconciles humanity.
- Christ, my reconciler.

We also were enemies of God. It was probably an unconscious antagonism, but it was real.

Note that verse 23 begins with a positive statement but also with a condition: "...provided that you continue..." (RSV); "...if you continue... (NIV).

7/ What is the promise and what is the condition?

Jesus Christ is Lord. Creator of the universe, both visible and invisible, and we know that all creation will submit itself to him at the assigned time. But we have the privilege of knowing him now as our Lord, and as we continue studying, we will find many practical applications of that reality. The members of a body function as they should when they are in close contact with the head, tuned in to its instructions. The lordship of Christ is something we live.

3 Paul's experience

⇨ Colosenses 1.24-2.5

Paul hadn't had a personal contact with the church in Colossae. Yet he had an indirect part in its formation and felt responsible towards it as an apostle of Christ. He wrote this passage to share his concern and his reasons for that concern.

Paul begins sharing his sufferings as a missionary. He gives details of his experience in other letters (such as in 2 Corinthians 11:23-33), but he says that in that way he shares the sufferings of Christ. From passages like Hebrews 7:27 and 1 Peter 3:18 we know that he is not referring to the sufferings of the cross since they were complete and adequate.

1/ Let's think about what verse 24 means.

a/ What relationship then could there be between the sufferings of Paul and those of Christ? Note John 15:20; Acts 9:16; Philippians 3:10; 2 Corinthians 1:4-7.

b/ How can Paul say "I rejoice in my sufferings"?

2/ Note that in 1:24 he speaks of "suffering for your sake", then in 2:1 he affirms that "I strive for your sake", and in 2:1 "I strive for you". They are expressions that imply that he was participating actively in that church.

a/ How can he say that when he did not know them personally? In what ways could he have participated in their church?

b/ How can we imitate this example of Paul today?

Nobody is an island: everything that we are, that we do or don't do affects other people. Paul was very aware of that. It is a conviction that we also should have.

3/ Besides this passage in Colossians, look at 1 Corinthians 12:26 and 2 Corinthians 1:4, 5 and complete this sentence:

I am not an island because...

A part of Paul's ministry was to proclaim the "mystery" of God (verse 26). The word "mystery" in the New Testament does not mean something that cannot be understood, but a secret that has been hidden. In that way there are things that were hidden to God's first people but that have been revealed with the coming of Jesus Christ.

4/ In this case, what is the mystery? Note also Ephesians 3:1-6.

The picture that Paul paints of his work is very dynamic, and we see a variety of dimensions of what he did. But it's important to note that he worked with a clear goal in mind.

5/ Note that in verse 27 Paul writes of "Christ in you". What effect should that have in your life?

6/ Taking into account this passage (1:24-2:3), what goals did Paul have in mind for this church?

Let's suppose that God has brought someone into your life who is a new believer, a Bill or Ruth that you ought to help in his or her Christian life. What can, or should you do to help that person grow? What does he or she need?

7/ Indicate some concrete steps that you could take to be a help.

Paul ends in 2:5 with an expression that reflects the unity of Christ's people. It is very probable that I do not know you, yet I feel a strong desire to see you grow. We have the same Spirit; we are brothers and sisters in the same family. And even though I am not present physically, in one sense I am with your study group. What the Lord wants is that we strive to see maturity in the people among whom we have a certain responsibility. May the Lord help us to be partakers, and not just observers of his work.

4 Our relationship with Christ

⇨ Colossians 2:6-15

Our tendency, as evangelicals, is to explain our relationship with Christ in a very limited way: "receive Christ", "have faith in Christ", etc. But in this passage Paul uses a language that is not very common for us and explores some of the profound dimensions of the new life in Christ.

Paul used two images to describe the Christian life: a plant and a building. They are images that we encounter a number of times in the Bible. For example, Jeremiah 17:5-8 speaks of a plant and Ephesians 2:20-22 of a building.

1/ What do these two images have in common?

Paul also warns us in this passage about certain heretics, false teachers who tried to disrupt the church in Colossae. The biblical commentators are not in agreement as to just what those errors were. But in any case, it is not necessary that we understand all the details in order to follow Paul's argument in this chapter. His reasoning still serves us in the defense of the Gospel.

There are two expressions in the passage that we should clarify:

- *Philosophy*. The word itself simply means "love of wisdom". In itself it is neither good or bad. Seeking the truth has value or not depending on our base thinking, our presuppositions.

- In verse 8 we find the "elemental spirits of the universe" (RSV), or of the "world" (ESV), "basic principles of the world" (NIV). The reference is probably to magical powers, astrology or the more primitive elements of religion that have been common during the history of humanity.

2/ What are the especially dangerous aspects of this menace?

3/ Are these dangers present today or are they in a different form?

4/ The "For..." in verse 9 explains why we should not be concerned. In what way do verses 9 and 10 give us a protection from the danger?

Starting with verse 11 Paul describes the Christian life by means of various comparisons.

5/ Is there a relationship between the circumcision Paul mentions in verse 11 and the baptism in verse 12? Do they describe the same thing?

The majority of us do not realize that both the first covenant made with Israel and the new covenant made with us were sealed by circumcision. Between the two there are differences, but there also are similarities.

We know that our sins were nailed with Jesus to the cross (1 Peter 2:24). But in verse 14 of this passage Paul says something different.

6/ What was nailed to the cross? Explain your answer.

At times when we study a passage like this one, we forget that it is speaking of you and I. It describes the profound changes that God has made in the life of each of his children, changes that should result in a different lifestyle. It is to that end that verse 6 challenges us and verse 8 warns us.

7/ To what conclusion should verses 11 to 14 lead us?

The passage ends with the figure of the victory parade of the Roman conquerors. After a victory in a war, the generals entered Rome with their troops and flags and with a great number of prisoners and spoils.

Paul claims that the victor this time is Christ. But what does he mean in verse 15? We still see the powers of darkness in action around us.

8/ How do you understand verse 15? If possible, find another biblical passage that supports your opinion.

In one sense what happened at the cross is simple: a man died. But at the same time that death has implications for all of humanity and for creation itself.

That gives us even more reason to pay special attention to the counsel of verses 6 and 7.

5 Legalism

⇨ Colossians 2:16-23

Up to this point Paul has gone against the ideas that were causing problems in the church at Colossae. He doesn't name them specifically, but he makes a clear stand for the supremacy of Jesus Christ and the need to have our roots deep in him. He stresses the need to avoid the man-made ideas that are not in accord with the revelation we have of Christ.

Now in this passage Paul deals with the practical consequences of these wrong teachings. Even though some details are not very clear, we can see the general form the problem takes, the same problem that appears presently in some Christian groups.

Note that this passage begins with "Therefore..." Which means that what Paul is saying here is a logical consequence of what he wrote earlier of the supremacy of Jesus Christ and our relationship with him.

In verse 16 Paul appears to describe the practice of the Jews who tried to retain their Judaism with their new faith in Christ.

1/ In what way were these Jewish practices a "shadow" of what was to come?

**2/ In verse 18 Paul warns of the possibility of being "disqualified".
Disqualified from what?**

**3/ Would there be a modern equivalent of the type of
"Christianity" described in verse 18?**

The problem with those people, says Paul, is that they have not
held themselves firm in Christ. They have been side-tracked, attracted
by what they imagined to be a higher level of spirituality.

The contrast in verse 18 is provocative. They "delight in false
humility" but at the same time are "puffed up" with their new ideas.
(NIV)

4/ How can a person live both extremes at the same time?

5/ How is it that the practices that Paul mentions in verses 16 and 21 are attractive for many people?

Starting with verse 20 Paul describes a form of legalism, that is, a Christian life surrounded by rules.

6/ Why, according to Paul, is that interpretation of the Christian life not valid?

7/ How do you interpret verse 22?

Paul says that the practices he has been describing have "an appearance of wisdom" but are "of no value" (verse 23 NIV).

8/ What does Paul mean by this?

9/ In this same passage we are now studying find the solutions to these problems that Paul has described (there are at least 3).

The dissenting faction of the church was concerned with the spiritual life of their brothers, and in that they meant well. But they had a problem discerning between "religiosity" and true spirituality. They wanted to impose practices that give the appearance of spirituality but that do not reach interior of a person, where true spirituality has its roots. In the following study we will see how Paul reveals the alternative to the position of the dissident group.

6 Old life, new life

⇨ Colossians 3:1-17

With this chapter Paul flips the coin and we can see the other side. To live a holy life has nothing to do with food, clothes, observation of holy days, etc. These things are all superficial. What God seeks is something much deeper. With this chapter Paul leads us on the path towards true holiness.

1/ The chapter begins on a positive note, in contrast to the legalism we saw in chapter 2.

a/ What does Paul challenge us to in verses 1-4?

b/ How do we apply these concepts (verses 1-4) in real life? Is it a life of contemplation? Is there something here that a person immersed in ten or more work hours a day can do?

Paul begins the chapter speaking of the "raised" life and from verse 5 on he gives us a series of factors as to how to live that life. He talks of things that should disappear from our lives, and others that should take their place.

2/ Of the list in verses 5-9, which of these wrongs appears worse
to you?

3/ In that same list, which appears least offensive? Why?

4/ We will look at only two items of that list in more detail.
   a/ Why would Paul say that greed, or covetousness, is a form
   of idolatry (verse 5)?

   b/ If to lie is to not tell the truth, then when we exaggerate
   something, we lie. Think of ways we can lie daily, without
   realizing it.

When we look at ourselves, and at our brothers in Christ, we realize that we are included in Paul's list; there are things in our lives that should have disappeared when we encountered Christ. And that reality leads us to the tension we see in this passage.

The Christian life is a constant tension. The Word of God speaks of the new life and we experience it, but at the same time that same Word acts like a mirror where we see there are still a lot of dark smudges on our face. The thinking Christian realizes that there is a contrast between what is and what should be; between the "new" man and the "old".

That is why we describe the Christian life as a process, a process of maturing that never ends in this life. We are on the way, arriving.

5/ If then, some of the things Paul mentions are still in our lives and should disappear, what does "put to death" such things (verse 5 RSV, ESV) or "put them away" (verse 8 RSV, ESV) mean? How do we do it? Be very realistic.

Though it is true that there are things in our lives that should disappear, the emphasis in the New Testament focuses on what God desires to form in us. The Christian life is not a "no" but a "yes". To give emphasis on the "no" creates emptiness, while the "yes" creates a new person.

Three times we encounter the expression "put on..." in this passage. We find it first in verse 10 where Paul speaks of the new life that becomes more and more like its creator. Then again in verse 12 he uses the expression to describe a series of attributes that should be ours.

Compare the qualities in verses 12 to 15 with the fruit of the Spirit in Galatians 5:22, 23. Note that there are various aspects that are repeated between the two lists.

6/ How much, then, does it depend on us to "put on" these things and how much does it depend on the Spirit?

We will finish this lesson with verse 16. Paul says that "we should teach and admonish one another in all wisdom." It is not an instruction for pastors but counsel for all of us.

7/ How do we do this?

Three times Paul says we should be thankful (verses 15, 16, 17).

8/ What personal motives do you have to be thankful, beyond the gift of your salvation?

Note that enormous word "everything" in verse 17. The message Christ brought is broad enough to cover all our life. Our relationship with Christ cannot just be an "important" part of our lives; it must be all.

In one sense the Christian life is like a jig-saw puzzle. Throughout life we are uniting different pieces in our experience and bit by bit a picture is formed. As we get towards the end, the picture that we thought would resemble us, looks like Christ.

Don't these verses give us ample motive to be thankful to our Father (verses 16 and 17)?

7 Us and our neighbor

⇨ Colossians 3:18-4:6

Our relationship with Jesus Christ shows itself in our homes, in the classroom, in the workplace. In this passage Paul gives specific instructions for various groups. All of us are included in at least one of them. In one sense, 3:17 is an introduction to this passage, since here we see how to put it into practice. Let's look at these persons and situations one by one.

Married couples (3:18, 19)

We cannot separate verses 18 and 19 since they are the two faces of the same coin. Note Ephesians 5:25 that clarifies verse 19.

1/ Explain in your own words what Paul requires of
   a/ husbands.

b/ wives.

c/ Of which of the two does Paul demand more? Explain your answer.

Parents and children (3:20, 21)

Again, we cannot separate verses 20 and 21. As in the first case they create a balance. Society has the tendency to treat a child with disrespect, as if they did not have their own rights.

2/ Do you think what Paul asks of children is fair, in other words, that there should never be any exceptions to this rule? Explain your answer.

3/ Verse 21 puts limits on what parents can do. How do you explain those limits?

Workers 3:22-25

Though the Greek word use here is "slave", the Bible commentators indicate that the principles Paul gives in this passage apply also to hired workers. Close to half of the workers in the Roman empire were slaves, and that included teachers and other professions. There was not that much difference between many slaves and free workers.

4/ How do we apply

    a/ verse 22?

    b/ verses 23 and 24?

    c/ verse 25?

5/ What should we do if we work for a dishonest person?

6/ If everyone where you work followed the guidelines laid down by Paul, what difference would there be in:

a/ The place where you work? (for students, study is your "work")

b/ the country where you live?

"Bosses" (4:1)

It is very likely that in the first churches there were many slaves and workers but few "bosses". Even among us there are not many who have people working for them.

7/ How can a person with authority apply what Paul says about doing things "justly and fairly"? What does that presently mean in practice?

Prayer (4:2-4)

Paul goes from specific relationships to general ones, from our responsibilities as fathers, sons and daughters, workers, etc. to two matters that are for every child of God. The first one is prayer.

8/ Verse 2 requests two things from us. ¿How do we apply them to our personal prayer?

Paul doesn't hesitate to request prayer for himself. He was very sure that he could not do anything without the power of God acting through him.

Those on the outside (4:5, 6)

This is one of the few passages in the Epistles that deal with our testimony towards those who are on the outside, that is, those who are not of Christ.

9/ Explain the following expressions in your own words:

    a/ "Conduct yourselves wisely..."

b/ "...making most of the time..."

c/ "...speech be gracious...seasoned with salt..."

The title of this lesson is "Us and our neighbor" since it gives us guidelines of conduct for our daily life, principles for our relationships with the people who surround us in our daily activities. It would be good to end with the words of our Lord: "If you know these things, blessed are you if you do them." (John 13:17)

8 Conclusion

⇨ Colossians 4:7-18

In this last portion we will encounter many names - some known, others not - who belonged to that widespread group of people who Paul maintained contact with. When we read the book of Acts, we realize that Paul always worked as part of a team. He never played the role of the solitary missionary; he was always accompanied by those who helped him and learned from him.

Let's see what we can learn from the eight people mentioned in verses 7 to 14. Your Bible may have information in its notes, or a concordance will help you find references to these names.

1/ What do we know of the following people:

a/ Tychicus

b/ Onesimus

c/ Aristarchus

d/ Jesus, called Justus

e/ Mark

f/ Epaphras

g/ Luke

h/ Demas

2/ From what we can see of these people, what do they have in
common to make them collaborators with Paul?

3/ As a final exercise we will make a global summary of the
letter. The divisions we have made in this study are listed below.
Make a summary of the principal ideas of each section.
   a/ 1:1-14

   b/ 1:15-23

   c/ 1:24-2:5

d/ 2:6-15

e/ 2:16-23

f/ 3-17

g/ 3:18-4.6

h/ 4:7-18

4/ If it is true, as the commentaries suggest, that Paul's main purpose in writing the letter was to combat certain errors that were entering the church,

    a/ What then was the error, or the principal errors?

    b/ What was Paul's main argument against these errors?

5/ Now that you have studied Paul's letter to the Colossae church, [see above] what is its message to you personally?

How to use this study

These studies are study guides, that is, their purpose is to guide you in your personal study of the subject or book of the Bible that the guide develops.

What the study proposes is a discussion. We introduce the theme, suggest how to proceed with the investigation, we comment, but we also ask. The spaces after the questions are for you to write in your answers.

We are hoping that with this give and take we help you to build your own understanding of the material. Not second hand, as when you listen to a sermon, but as fruit of your own reading and investigation.

How to do the study?

1 – Before you start, pray. Ask God that he might speak to you and give you understanding during your study.

2 – When there is a Bible passage, read it more than one time and ask yourself: What is the writer trying to say? Even though many use the King James version of the Bible it would be good to have other versions available, so you can compare scripture with scripture. The Revised Standard Version, the New International Version or others can help you see the passage of scripture with more clarity.

3 – Do the lesson. Try your best to make as clear an answer as possible. Don't hurry just to finish. It is better to go carefully, thinking, asking, clarifying.

With the group

Personal study is important, but its value increases if it is accompanied with study in a group. A group of up to 8 people is ideal, but if the group is only you and one other person it is still better than studying alone.

Actually these studies have been designed with this purpose: to stimulate the study of the Bible in small groups. The system to use is simple:

1 – **Do one of the chapters on your own**. Even if there are things you don't understand, do your best to finish the chapter.

2 – **Meet with the group**. In the group you share the answers to each question. It is very possible that you will not all have the same answers, but then by comparing the results among the entire group you can clarify and if necessary correct your answer.

It is the discussion above all that provides the greatest benefit of this system of study.

3 – **Avoid getting off the subject**. It is easy to get distracted by personal issues or arguments about some particular question. If an important issue comes up you can dedicate a special session of the group to handle it.

4 – **Participate**. Everyone should take part. It is that which gives value to the study in group.

5 – **Listen**. We often have the tendency to jump in with our own conclusions before we allow the other person to finish. We will learn from each other, even from those, who in our opinion, are wrong.

6 – **Don't dominate the discussion**. It may be that you have the study down pat, yet it is important that you give space to others and encourage the possibly timid person to take part.

May the Lord help you in this task, and if you need help we are ready to assist you. Feel free to contact us.

Other titles in English

Growing in Faith!
José Young

This study is for the new believer. It covers essential aspects of the christian life, basic matters that a son of God should know and practice from the beginning of life in Christ. God wants us to grow, and that brings us to his book, the Bible, where we find the keys for that growth.

Ediciones Crecimiento Cristiano is in the process of translating it's studies to English.

Some of the first titles:

- **John's letters,** In this we know love
- **The Gospel of John,** Behold the Lamb of God
- **The Gospel according to Mark,** Who is this man?
- **James,** Faith that works
- **Tito,** The fruitful life
- **The Sermon on the Mount,** But I tell you…